THE WEATHERING GRACE OF GOD

THE WEATHERING GRACE OF GOD

The Beauty God Brings From Life's Upheavals

KEN GIRE

Servant Publications
Ann Arbor, Michigan

Vine Books is an imprint of Servant Publications especially designed to
serve evangelical Christians.

Unless otherwise credited, Scripture quotations are from the New
American Standard Bible, © The Lockman Foundation 1960, 1962,
1963, 1968, 1971, 1973, 1975, 1977. Verses marked (NIV) are taken
from the HOLY BIBLE, NEW INTERNATIONAL VERSION®.
Copyright 1973, 1978, 1984 by International Bible Society. Used by
permission of Zondervan Publishing House. All rights reserved. Verses
marked (KJV) are from the King James Version.

Published by Servant Publications
P.O. Box 8617
Ann Arbor, Michigan 48107

Cover design: Uttley/Douponce DesignWorks, Sisters, Oregon

02 03 04 10 9 8 7 6 5 4 3

Printed in the United States of America
ISBN 1-56955-221-5

Library of Congress Cataloging-in-Publication Data

Gire, Ken
   The weathering grace of God : the beauty God brings from life's
upheavals / Ken Gire.
       p. cm.
   ISBN 1-56955-221-5 (alk. paper)
   1. Suffering—Religious aspects—Christianity. 2. Nature—Religious
aspects—Christianity. I. Title.
   BV4909 .G57 2001
   248.8'6—dc21

                                                           2001004349

For

Jack and Leesa
and
Craig and Alese

With Love

ACKNOWLEDGMENTS

This was a difficult book for me.
It was also a difficult book
for my editor, Kathy Deering.
Her patience with me was exceeded
only by her kindness toward me.
Thank you, Kathy, for both.

He makes everything beautiful in its time.

Solomon

ECCLESIASTES 3:11

THE WEATHERING GRACE OF GOD

CONTENTS

Thou who wouldst see the lovely and the wild
Mingled in harmony on Nature's face,
Ascend our rocky mountains.

William Cullen Bryant
From his poem, "Monument Mountain"

PROLOGUE

When we draw close to Nature, reaching out to it for clues to our existence, Nature takes our hands and fills them with the fertile loam of our humanity, reminding us that from the earth we were taken and to the earth we will return.

It's humbling to realize for us who have been given dominion over Nature how limited that dominion is. We can light candles, but we can't hold back the night. We can prepare for storms, but we can't prevent them. We can't stop the rains in times of flood or start them in times of drought. We can't shorten winter or lengthen spring.

In Nature we are confronted with the limits of our dominion. Nowhere are those limits so obvious as in the way mountains are formed. When sheer formations of rock are suddenly thrust through the surface of the earth,

we are helpless to stop it. Helpless to control either its duration or its devastation.

We are just as helpless when some tragedy devastates us. Like the death of a child. Or the diagnosis of a cancer. The prodigal who runs away from home. Or the partner who walks away from the marriage. The sudden disability from a wreck. Or the sobering dismissal from work.

Upheavals come suddenly, unexpectedly, and often catastrophically. Whenever they come, however they come, they forever alter the settled terrain that once was our life. Embedded within us are physical, spiritual, and psychological layers that make up our interior landscape. When upheavals come, they alter every layer with varying degrees of destruction that sometimes take a lifetime to unearth.

Imagine for a minute that *you* are the landscape. The upheaval thrusts itself mercilessly through the very center of who you are. The abrading of granite. The crumbling of

limestone. The crashing of boulders as they tumble down around you, shattering to pieces. You feel all of that, every grinding moment of it. Your stomach drops, your head spins, and you watch in helpless horror as the innermost parts of your life lie on the surface, exposed to the elements.

The deafening noise is the sound of the upheaval as it forces its way through every stratified layer that lies within you. Your body, mind, emotions, all these layers are displaced. They are folded or pushed upward or thrust over each other. The social layers of your life are also shaken. And the spiritual layers that once seemed such bedrock certainties, they're shaken, too.

Who of us can survive the shock and aftershocks of such earthshaking experiences? Who of us has the strength to sift through the emotional rubble of the resulting devastation? Who of us has the courage to face the future where other upheavals may await us?

THE WEATHERING GRACE OF GOD

Meanwhile, where is God in all of this? Didn't He see the upheaval coming? Couldn't He have prevented it? Or at least warned us of it?

Much the way pressure within the earth thrusts rock formations through its crust to create mountains, the seismic pressure of these unanswered questions creates sudden and sometimes terrifying upheavals in our faith.

To this bare and broken rock, God comes.

There the weathering grace of God begins its work, wearing granite into soil, planting windblown seeds into barren slopes, bringing life out of lifelessness, beauty out of ugliness.

Season after season, the work continues.

In time, God turns the most terrifying of eruptions into the most majestic of mountains, the most tragic of earthquakes into the most idyllic of landscapes.

That is the unrelenting work of heaven, to make everything beautiful in its time.

PROLOGUE

Dear Lord,

I believe You are a sovereign God,
  Creator of the heavens and the earth.

I believe You are ruler of the universe
  and Lord of the landscape of my life.

However small a parcel of ground
  that is within Your universe,
    it is still within Your universe,
      and still under Your watchful eye.

I believe You know what happens there,
  and that You care what happens there,
    especially in times of upheaval.

THE WEATHERING GRACE OF GOD

I believe You are good,
*   and work all things for good*
*   to those who love You*
*   and are called according to Your purpose.*

I believe You are all-powerful,
*   and that You make everything beautiful in its time.*

All these things, I believe, Lord.
Help my unbelief.

All Nature's wildness tells the same story: the shocks and outbursts of earthquakes, volcanoes, geysers, roaring, thundering waves and floods, the silent uprush of sap in plants, storms of every sort, each and all, are the orderly, beauty-making love-beats of Nature's heart.

John Muir
"Three Adventures in the Yosemite"
Century Magazine, March 1912

THE TERRIFYING
UPHEAVALS OF LIFE

I love the mountains, especially the Rocky Mountains. I have loved them since my first vacation to Colorado as a young boy. They seem so regal with their shoulder capes of snow, ruling from such lofty thrones. Just being in their presence is ennobling. When sitting with them, I feel as if I have been seated at some royal table, a common knave in the company of kings.

I come to these mountains for a lot of reasons. To get away from the phone is one. And from the computer. And the incremental nag of the organizer that minces my day, telling me where I should be and when, what I should be doing and for how long. I come for exercise. And solitude. I come to give my thoughts room to wander, uncinching them so they can go off grazing by themselves, without me guiding them or chiding them.

THE WEATHERING GRACE OF GOD

The mountain I'm hiking is somewhere around 8,000 feet. The air up here is crisp and clean but also thin. I stop against an outcropping of rock to let my breath catch up. A stream passes beneath me, scalloped with sunlight. Crumblings of granite, called skree, are strewn over the ground, a transitional link from the pinkish gray of the rock to the pinkish brown of the soil. A few tired trees lean diagonally against the tall brown strength of other trees. A giant of a pine lies lifeless on the ground, tethered there by the Lilliputian forces of the forest, patiently awaiting its decay.

I continue up the coarsely cut road to where it dwindles to a path, then a footpath. I pass a sign that tells me I am entering "Rocky Mountain National Park." Everything is still, like held breath. The only sound is the wind mussing tops of trees. Walking farther, I find myself surrounded by a hushed conclave of boulders so huge they dwarf everything around them. In the silence I can hear myself breathing,

THE TERRIFYING UPHEAVALS OF LIFE

feel my heart pounding. I find a grassy spot on the downward slope of the mountain and sit to take in the view. Across the way is another row of peaks, serrated against the sky like the great, fossilized back of some fallen dinosaur.

So captivating is the view, I can hardly think about anything else. The poet, William Cullen Bryant, who was also captivated by the Rocky Mountains, wrote:

> Let thy foot
> Fail not with weariness, for on their tops
> The beauty and majesty of earth,
> Spread wide beneath, shall make thee to forget
> The steep and toilsome way.

He was right. The beauty and majesty of these mountains did make me forget the steep and toilsome hike it took to get here. They also made me remember *why* I came.

THE WEATHERING GRACE OF GOD

I feel closer to God up here. That is a big reason why I came, why I always come. The mountains are so conducive to His company. The distant peaks seem the spires of some ancient cathedral. The tall pines seem on their way to worship there, but they have stopped, as if part of some solemn monastic order, pausing for their hour of prayer.

Sitting up here, much more than by gazing up here from the foothills, I understand why mountains have captured the spiritual imagination of so many civilizations throughout history.

The Bible records a number of such instances. Pagan religions placed their altars and shrines in the high mountains (Deuteronomy 12:1-3). Mountains are often referred to, figuratively, as the dwelling place of God (Psalm 68: 15-16). It is to His dwelling place in these mountains that we are called to look for help in times of need (Psalm 121:1). Mountains are associated with sacrifice (Mount

THE TERRIFYING UPHEAVALS OF LIFE

Moriah, Genesis 22), with testing (Mount Carmel, 1 Kings 18:20-46), with revelation (Mount Sinai, Exodus 19:17–20:21; Mount Horeb, 1 Kings 19:8-18), and with worship (Mount Gerizim and Mount Zion, John 4:19-21).

More recently, these majestic peaks captured the spiritual imagination of a man named John Muir. An ardent conservationist, Muir was the most renowned mountaineer in U.S. history. And the most respected. For a period of twenty-five years in the late 1800s, he set physical standards for climbing that are hard to believe for a man who used no ropes or climbing tools, carried no tent or camping equipment.

Taking with him the most Spartan of provisions—a little bread, tea, oatmeal, and a blanket or two—Muir climbed many of the major peaks of North America, including Mount McKinley, Mount Shasta, Mount Rainier, Mount Ritter, and the subrange of peaks south of Yosemite.

THE WEATHERING GRACE OF GOD

Muir often climbed alone, even in below-zero weather. The thin air and mountain foliage seemed to intoxicate him. He brought to the sport of climbing not only a love for Nature but also a philosophy that saw within Nature the beauty of God's designs.

Raised a strict Calvinist, Muir had memorized all of the New Testament and three quarters of the Old by the time he was eleven. He could, in fact, recite the entire New Testament without stopping. As he grew older, he left his religious roots, though he never abandoned his love for God or his awe for God's handiwork. He saw beauty everywhere, from the grandest peaks to the smallest crystals.

With the apostle Paul, John Muir believed that the natural creation revealed the power and majesty of God (Romans 1:20). Muir's experience of God in creation was so real that sharing it became an evangelistic obsession. "Heaven knows," he said, "that John the Baptist was not

more eager to get all his fellow sinners into the Jordan than I to baptize all of mine in the beauty of God's mountains."

Muir didn't always feel this way about God's mountains, though. In 1866, he moved to the industrial city of Indianapolis, intent on becoming an inventor. In his childhood he had built clocks, thermometers, a barometer, and a combination lock from ordinary household materials. Though his neighbors ogled over his accomplishments, his sternly religious father refrained from praising him for fear it might lure the boy toward the sin of pride.

Arriving in Indianapolis, Muir secured employment at a large machine shop, where his work distinguished him so much that the owners wanted to bring him into the firm as a partner. Shortly before the owners made their offer, an accident happened. A metal file Muir was working with slipped and punctured his eye. He lost sight in

that eye, and his other eye went into a state of "sympathetic" blindness.

Entering this nether world of darkness, Muir fell into an abyss of depression. Gradually he recovered his sight. As he did, he recovered something else, a new appreciation for the gift God had returned to him. During this time a transformation was taking place within him, and he felt on the verge of finding some new mission for his life. While he was convalescing in bed, looking through a brochure of the Yosemite valley, that mission became clear.

Visiting the recuperating Muir, the owners offered him a partnership. He turned it down. In a letter to a friend, he explained why.

"As soon as I got out into Heaven's light I started on another long excursion, making haste with all my heart to store my mind with the Lord's beauty and thus be ready for any fate, light or dark. And it was

THE TERRIFYING UPHEAVALS OF LIFE

from this time that my long continuous wanderings may be said to have fairly commenced. I bade adieu to all my mechanical inventions, determined to devote the rest of my life to the study of the inventions of God."

Muir's blindness was an upheaval in the landscape of his life. The upheaval plunged him into physical and emotional darkness. In time he emerged from the darkness, seeing the world through different eyes. With his vision restored and his passion renewed, Muir set about exploring the beauty of the great alpine wonders of North America. He later founded a society of conservationists called the Sierra Club. He also worked tirelessly to preserve Nature's wonders and helped to turn many of them into national parks. Through his speaking and writing, he returned a spiritual dimension to Nature that for so long had been lost to Christianity.

THE WEATHERING GRACE OF GOD

Muir's life was filled with long pilgrimages to the mountains he loved. Some of them were monastic stints where he sauntered off by himself. Others were taken in the company of friends. He referred to mountains as "the manuscripts of God," an allusion to the title of a poem by Henry Longfellow:

And nature, the old nurse, took
  The child upon her knee,
Saying, "Here is a story book
  My father hath writ for thee.
Come, wander with me," she said,
  "In regions yet untrod
And read what is still unread
  In the manuscripts of God."

Having studied those divine texts, Muir used them to proclaim the glory of God. He was a prophet, of sorts, and

did what prophets do best—help people to see and to understand.

I am one of those people.

He helped me to see what is beautiful.

And to understand that the first stage of beautiful is upheaval.

I was browsing a bookstore one day when I happened upon a topographical map of Colorado, molded in plastic. A yellow line representing Interstate 25 ran down the center,

dividing the map in half. I stooped to pick it up and ran my fingers across its surface. The eastern half had barely a dimple on the landscape. The western half had peaks and valleys that formed the southern range of the Rocky Mountains.

Though I live near that concrete seam dividing the state, I had never seen where I live from that perspective. The contrast was striking. The even terrain of eastern Colorado was smooth to the touch. The uncertain terrain of western Colorado was bumpy.

The map intrigued me, so much so that I bought it and took it home. I thought about it a lot. It seemed to be a parable of some kind. Nature is as full of parables as a mountain is with wildflowers, each holding a secret that can't be forced. Slowly, over the days that followed, the petals of that parable unfolded.

Eastern and western Colorado.

Smooth, even terrain ... and bumpy, uncertain terrain.

THE TERRIFYING UPHEAVALS OF LIFE

Life as we would like it ... and life as we are given it.

The physical landscape was a metaphor of the landscape of our lives. One had no upheavals. The other was full of them.

If the contrasting landscapes represented two different ways of life, which landscape, I wondered, would I pick for mine?

Eastern Colorado, of course. At least, that was my initial response. Then I thought about it. I thought about how flat and featureless eastern Colorado is. And I realized ...

Nobody comes to eastern Colorado for a vacation.

They all come to western Colorado.

They come to hike and to camp and to fish. They come to ski and to sightsee. They come to take pictures so they can savor the experience themselves and share it with others.

Why do they come? I wondered.

Beauty, I think, is what draws them. Looking from the

THE WEATHERING GRACE OF GOD

back deck of my house, I take in the beauty of the panoramic sweep of the Front Range. My eyes linger on the highest mountain, Pike's Peak. It is so peaceful here. As I reflect upon its origins, though, I realize that this landscape wasn't always beautiful, and living here wasn't always peaceful.

Once this was the most terrifying place in all of Colorado to live.

At the onset of the great Flood, the earth's crust fractured, releasing subterranean reservoirs of water (Genesis 7:11). The fractures broke the earth into massive tectonic plates and sent them drifting as continents. As the floodwaters receded, the earth convulsed (Psalm 104:1-8). Gripping contractions within the earth pushed great formations of rock to crown its surface. The sounds of labor were deafening. If you lived here, you would have fled for your life, if your life had even survived the ordeal. With a grating scream and one final push, the Rocky Mountains

THE TERRIFYING UPHEAVALS OF LIFE

were born, and a great granite nakedness lay shivering on the earth's surface.

What a price to pay for beauty. Was it worth it, I wonder? Was the majestic beauty of the Rockies worth the terrifying upheavals that produced them?

An unqualified *yes*.

But then, I'm the one on the back deck, admiring the view ... not the one in labor, giving birth.

▼▲▼▼▲▼

The upheaval came one quiet afternoon when I was alone. It came in the form of a phone call from a friend. Her first sentence was an uninflected greeting. Her second sentence started with the name of a close friend's son,

followed by the word "suicide." I can't remember another word after that word. I only remember crying, "Oh, no. Oh, God, no, no, no."

I hung up the phone and slumped to the bed. My body trembled, my chest heaved. "Oh, no. Oh, God, no," I moaned, over and over and over. "Oh, God, no, no." I couldn't stop crying and shaking.

I called Judy at work. "I need you to come home."

"What's the matter?"

My voice crumbled. "I just need you to come home, now."

"Is it your mom?"

"No," I answered, crying.

"What's the matter? You have to tell me what's the matter," she insisted. "Is it one of the kids?"

"No." And then I told her.

Twenty minutes later, she arrived. Meeting her at the door were a couple of close friends. We held each other and

THE TERRIFYING UPHEAVALS OF LIFE

cried. I couldn't stop trembling, though. Or weeping. Or moaning. "He was just a kid. He was just a kid."

I never cried so hard or so long in my life. The two friends hugged me and stood by me until it seemed the tears had run their course. Then the phone rang. Judy answered it. It was the boy's father, asking for me. The weight of his name, when Judy said it, bent me over on the kitchen counter, spilling out more tears. Judy led me to the phone in the other room.

I didn't have the strength to face the friend's voice. "Oh, God," I pleaded, "please help me, please. Please help me."

I pushed myself to the phone, still sobbing. My friend told me the details in as few words as I could bear to hear. After he said goodbye, I sat on the side of the bed, quiet and empty and still.

My friend and his wife had been at the hospital when each of our children were born, and my wife and I had been at the hospital when each of theirs were. We had known

the boy who committed suicide since the day of his birth. We had watched him grow up, some years up close, other years from a distance. Our children knew him. One of our daughters had been in the same classroom with him at school. More recently, he had stayed with us several days during a snowstorm on his way home.

We drove to the funeral, where Scriptures were read and explanations were given. An all-things-work-together-for-good hope was extended to the family. The words were addressed to the father, mostly because it was the father that most of these men knew. You will become a better preacher because of this, a better writer, too.

I believe the men were sincere and their words true. I believe the family will emerge from this a closer family, a stronger family. I believe the father indeed will become a better preacher and a better writer.

Given the choice, though, this father would have settled for being less of a preacher and less of a writer.

THE TERRIFYING UPHEAVALS OF LIFE

But he was not given the choice.

He would have given up the books he had already written and the sermons he had already preached.

But he was not given that choice.

He would have given his own life. He was not given that choice, either.

The trip back to Colorado was long and quiet and crowded with thoughts. When I arrived home, it was to the only partially finished book you are now reading. I didn't want to finish it, partly because I didn't have the energy to finish it, but partly, too, because I didn't want to be partner to a platitude. I didn't want to write and tell people about the beauty God brings from the upheavals in our lives when I couldn't see so much as a sprig of beauty coming from this. I didn't want to write, not just on this book, but ever again.

A terrible thing had happened. For whatever reason, God had allowed the human will to go forward,

THE WEATHERING-GRACE OF GOD

unchecked, with all its frightful consequences. He had allowed the will of the Enemy to go forward, too, unchecked, too, with all of its frightful consequences.

Why?

I can't answer that. And if I could, I wouldn't. At least not to the family.

If an earthquake were to destroy your house, and you were sitting among the rubble, battered from the falling debris and bleeding from the shattered glass, crying out "why," what comfort would there be in someone giving you a geological answer for what happened?

Or in this case, a theological one?

There are times, and this was one of those times, that I wished I didn't believe in God. It seemed if we took God out of the picture, we wouldn't take the upheavals so personally. And though the upheavals might still destroy the landscape of our lives, at least they wouldn't kick up the cosmic dust that causes us to spend a lot of time wandering in its haze,

THE TERRIFYING UPHEAVALS OF LIFE

disoriented and trying to make some kind of sense of it.

It would be so much easier just to say that the world is filled with randomness and chaos and bad things happen to all of us, and we should just enjoy what we can of life, thanking our lucky stars that bad things don't happen to us more often than they do.

In some ways I have recovered from the experience. In other ways I have not. I wonder what all was lost besides this boy who died too young. I wonder what was lost to the family, to their friends, and to our family who knew the boy, cared about him, prayed for him.

Before we left for the funeral, my wife, our one daughter, and I were sitting on the bed together, talking, and our daughter's tearful feelings came spilling out: "I just don't get it ... I mean, why pray? What's the use of praying for someone all these years if it just ends like this? I just want to give up. What's the use?"

THE WEATHERING GRACE OF GOD

I wondered those same things. I wondered what possible beauty could come out of such a tragedy. And I wondered at what price it would come.

Too great a price, if you ask me.

Would any of it *ever* come?

Someday, maybe.

But not today, not for me anyway.

THE TERRIFYING UPHEAVALS OF LIFE

Today I am back in Colorado, where I hear on the nightly news that an earthquake of 7.6 magnitude has just devastated the Central American country of El Salvador. So far, more than seven hundred dead have been found. Hundreds more are missing. Thousands of homes were destroyed, and thousands more lives devastated.

The quake happened on a Saturday at 11:35 in the morning. At that moment, the mountain overlooking the town of Santa Tecla began to shake, lightly at first, then more vigorously. The first thing anyone heard was a blood-curdling scream from a man guarding an expensive mansion nested near the mountaintop.

Then came the jolt. In one terrifying second, the entire hillside collapsed, sending an avalanche of dirt to the town below. The one thousand-foot-wide path of destruction buried three hundred homes in three stories of dirt.

Among the missing were three five-year-olds who were riding the bicycles they had received on Christmas, a

45

THE WEATHERING GRACE OF GOD

woman walking to the market for a carton of eggs, and a twelve-year-old boy who was sitting at home, waiting for a phone call from his father who lived in the United States.

Among those mourning was Miguel Ortega. He had been caring for his horses on his ranch when the quake struck. He sprinted home to see if his wife and three sons were safe. When he arrived, his property had been buried with so much dirt it took him several minutes before he could even find his house. Once he did, he fell to his knees and wept. Only the family dog survived.

One minute a well-guarded mansion was a fortress, a safe haven for its wealthy American owner. The next minute, it was shaken to its foundations. One minute the home of Miguel Ortega was his family's shelter. The next minute, it was their coffin.

How does anyone survive such upheavals? How will Miguel Ortega survive? How will my friends? And how

THE TERRIFYING UPHEAVALS OF LIFE

will they ever find the strength to sift through all the layers of destruction, layers that may take a lifetime to unearth?

▼▲▼▼▲▼

Living in southern California for seven years, our family experienced a number of earthquakes. None of them were like the one in El Salvador. Most merely set your nerves on edge. A few caused damage, but unless you lived at the epicenter, the damage was minimal. Some of the earthquakes felt as if you were on a raft with an ocean swell rolling beneath you. Others felt as if you were sitting in a chair and someone came up behind you, lifted the chair, and slammed it to the floor. Those were the worst.

THE WEATHERING GRACE OF GOD

One of those quakes came during a morning when the kids were getting ready for school and I was getting ready for work. After the first tremor, I turned on the news to see what had happened. A reporter was describing the incident when suddenly the newsroom started shaking. Our house started shaking, too, and we called to the children to take cover. The shaking grew worse, scaring the reporter, who ducked under his desk. The TV went black a second before the quake jolted our house, rattling everything in it, including us.

It was a terrifying experience. Part of the terror was not knowing how long the earthquake would last or how bad it might get. It lasted an eternity, or so it seemed. In reality, it was less than a minute. For those of us who lived in Fullerton, the damage wasn't serious. For those in Whittier, though, entire houses were lifted off their foundations, cracking walls, shattering glass, rupturing water lines and gas lines, opening crevasses in the concrete.

THE TERRIFYING UPHEAVALS OF LIFE

Again, nothing like the upheaval in El Salvador.
Or the upheavals in Psalm 46.

God is our refuge and strength,
A very present help in trouble.
Therefore we will not fear, though the earth should
    change,
And though the mountains slip into the heart of the
    sea;
Though its waters roar and foam,
Though the mountains quake at its swelling pride.
                                                    [Selah]

There is a river whose streams make glad the city of
    God,
The holy dwelling places of the Most High.
God is in the midst of her, she will not be moved;
God will help her when morning dawns.

THE WEATHERING GRACE OF GOD

The nations made an uproar, the kingdoms tottered;
He raised His voice, the earth melted.
The Lord of Hosts is with us;
The God of Jacob is our stronghold.

[Selah]

Come, behold the works of the Lord,
Who has wrought desolations in the earth.
He makes wars to cease to the end of the earth;
He breaks the bow and cuts the spear in two;
He burns the chariots with fire.
"Cease striving and know that I am God;
I will be exalted among the nations, I will be exalted
in the earth."
The Lord of Hosts is with us;
The God of Jacob is our stronghold.

[Selah]

THE TERRIFYING UPHEAVALS OF LIFE

The psalm consists of three stanzas. Verses 2-3 of the first stanza frame a picture of natural upheavals, where the earth gives way and the mountains fall into the sea, where the waters roar and the mountains quake. Verse 6 of the second stanza frames a picture of political upheavals, where nations are in uproar and kingdoms are in collapse. Verse 9 frames a picture of military upheavals, where God intervenes to break the bow, shatter the spear, and burn the shields with fire.

The pictures from the psalm form a composite of how uncertain life is and how terrifying it can become. One minute an embassy building is a safe haven for those seeking asylum. The next minute, a terrorist bomb reduces the embassy to rubble. One minute Jerusalem is a city of peace. The next minute, its streets are filled with gunfire from Israeli soldiers and their Palestinian neighbors. One minute Mount St. Helens stands as a sturdy silhouette against the Washington state skies. The next minute, it

THE WEATHERING GRACE OF GOD

explodes, ripping away half the mountain, laying waste 150 square miles of forest, and blanketing the state with volcanic ash.

For you and me, it may not be a natural disaster we fear, but it might be a moral one. It may not be a political collapse that worries us, but it might be a physical one. It may not be a military battle that is scaring us, but it might be a marital one.

Surviving these upheavals often depends on very basic things. When we used to live along the webwork of fault lines running beneath southern California, we were exposed to a lot of earthquake survival procedures. One of those procedures was to stay still. Most injuries, we were told, didn't come from the earthquake but from people trying to escape the earthquake. As they scramble out of the building they're in, many slip and fall, others are hit by flying glass or falling debris. Some, in their panic, suffer heart attacks.

THE TERRIFYING UPHEAVALS OF LIFE

The advice of professionals is to stay calm and be still. That is also the advice of Psalm 46. "Cease striving" (v. 10a). The Hebrew word means to relax, to let the hand release its grip, to let the body go slack, to be still.

In his book of Sabbath poems, titled, *A Timbered Choir*, Wendell Berry describes what happens when we are still.

> *The mind that comes to rest is tended*
> *In ways that it cannot intend:*
> *Is borne, preserved, and comprehended*
> *By what it cannot comprehend.*

Poets know the importance of this kind of stillness. They know that if they are still enough, long enough, the art they are working on will speak to them, tell them what it wants to be and what it needs from them to become it. All artists know this, whether they work with paint or clay, words or musical notes.

THE WEATHERING GRACE OF GOD

Michelangelo knew how to be still before the stone and listen to the David within it. Strauss knew how to be still before the Danube and listen to the waltz that was eddying about in its waters. Monet knew how to be still before the pond and listen to the lilies sunning on its surface.

What we are asked to listen to in times of upheaval is the voice of the Great Artist Himself, who will one day bring, out of the upheavals in this world, a new heaven and a new earth. And who is in the process of bringing, out of the upheavals in our life, a new heaven and new earth within us as well.

Our culture knows little of this kind of listening. That is true of our religious culture as well.

In his book, *The Pursuit of God*, A. W. Tozer wrote:

Religion has accepted the monstrous heresy that noise, size, activity and bluster make a man dear to God. But we may take heart. To a people caught in

THE TERRIFYING UPHEAVALS OF LIFE

the tempest of the last great conflict God says, "Be still, and know that I am God" (Psalm 46:10), and still He says it, as if He means to tell us that our strength and safety lie not in noise but in silence.

Again, the insight of poet Wendell Berry:

Best of any song
is bird song
in the quiet, but first
you must have the quiet.

Best of any voice is the voice of God, especially in times of upheaval. But other voices clamor for our attention in times like these. Inner voices, mostly. Voices of denial, of doubt, disillusionment, despair. Voices that are anxious and fearful, anguished and regretful. Loud and insistent voices that drown out the voice of God.

THE WEATHERING GRACE OF GOD

A poet, one like Henry Wadsworth Longfellow, knows that to hear this best of voices, we first must have the quiet.

Let us then labour for an inward stillness,
An inward stillness and an inward healing,
That perfect silence where the lips and heart
   are still,
And we no longer entertain our own imperfect
   Thought and vain opinions,
But God above speaks in us,
And we wait in singleness of heart,
That we may know His will,
And in the silence of our spirit
That we may do His will,
And do that only ...

THE TERRIFYING UPHEAVALS OF LIFE

In stillness we are offered a sacrament—the knowledge of God.

Not knowledge *about* God.

Knowledge *of* God.

"No amount of wordmaking," said John Muir, "will make a single soul to *know* these mountains.... One day's exposure to these mountains is better than cartloads of books."

Our study of God will not prepare us for the upheavals of life.

Only our experience of God will do that.

Theology, which is the study of God, is largely a bookish endeavor, undertaken from the sequestered safety of a study. It is not an adventure. It is an analysis of the adventures of others.

It is one thing to study Mount Everest.

It is another thing to scale it.

It is one thing to study the stories of those who have

ascended its heights. To draw general principles from those stories. And to make personal applications from them.

It's another thing to scale its cliffs and struggle for footholds. To brave the cold and endure the pain. To risk falling and freezing to death.

In the parking lot at the trailhead to the Palmer Lake Reservoir is a sign that reads: "Hike at Your Own Risk." To know God is to encounter the mountain. We hike at our own risk. That is why Jesus says to count the cost before leaving base camp. Because when we do leave, everything is at risk. Our safety is at risk. Our time is at risk. Our money. Our reputation. Our job, our relationships, everything.

In the context of Psalm 46, when our very lives are at risk, we are offered the knowledge of God. Who *is* this God we are asked to know?

Twice in the psalm is the refrain: "The Lord Almighty is with us; / the God of Jacob is our fortress" (vv. 7, 11).

THE TERRIFYING UPHEAVALS OF LIFE

"The Lord Almighty"

"The God of Jacob"

The images are comforting. The pairing within the images, though, is confusing. You would expect "the Lord Almighty" to be "our fortress" and "the God of Jacob" to be "with us." Here it is just the opposite. The Lord Almighty who commands the armies of Heaven, He is not pictured as our fortress. It is the God of Jacob, the God who draws near to us, who speaks to us, loves us, enters into a relationship with us. *He* is our fortress.

The Hebrew word for fortress comes from the root that means "to be high" and, by extension, "to be safe." It is used throughout the psalms of God as a rock, a refuge, and a fortress (Psalm 62:2, 71:3). From it we get the word "Masada," which was the desert fortress of Herod the Great. Rising 1,300 feet in the dry desert air, this rugged, flat-topped mountain faces the western shore of the Dead Sea. It was first fortified by the high priest Jonathan

THE WEATHERING GRACE OF GOD

somewhere between 103 and 76 B.C. Herod the Great later claimed it, transforming it into a palatial hideaway.

According to the Jewish historian Josephus, Herod furnished Masada as a refuge for himself in case of insurrection by the Jews or invasion by Cleopatra of Egypt. With its high summit and sheer cliffs, it was virtually impregnable. Masada was built as a retreat, but it served as a refuge in case of political upheavals.

Our intimacy with the Lord is our Masada.

That is our place of refuge. That is our source of strength. That is our very present help in time of trouble.

Masadas are not built in times of trouble. They are peace-time projects, built and fortified in times of stability. If we wait until the upheaval to begin building, there won't be a fortress to run to when we need to.

The disciples are a case in point.

During the upheaval that led to Christ's crucifixion, the disciples fell away from Him in reverse order of their

intimacy with Him. First was Judas, the one who had the least intimate relationship with Christ. After Judas' betrayal, the other disciples scattered. The three who had the most intimate relationship with Jesus were Peter, James, and John.

Of the twelve, John had the most intimate relationship.

At the Last Supper, John was the disciple sitting next to Jesus, leaning his head against the Savior's chest (John 13:23). At the tomb, he was the first disciple to believe that Jesus had been resurrected (John 20:1-16). At the Sea of Galilee, he was the disciple who first recognized Jesus' voice (John 21:1-7).

We are not told what happened to James the night that Jesus was betrayed. But Peter, he followed Jesus as far as the courtyard of the high priest before he fell away. Only John, the disciple whom Jesus loved, followed him all the way to the Cross.

At the Cross, John witnessed the most compelling sermon

on love ever preached. It is no wonder that forty percent of the New Testament's teaching on love came from this disciple. It is no wonder that to him Jesus entrusted the care of his mother (John 19:26-27). And it is no wonder that years later Jesus entrusted to him the greatest revelation ever given a human being (Revelation 1:9-19).

John's love for Christ is what drew him close.

It is also what kept him close.

And it is what became his refuge, his strength, and his very present help in time of trouble.

THE TERRIFYING UPHEAVALS OF LIFE

I don't know what it would be like to lose a child. The pain, the fear, the emptiness, the loneliness, the despair. I can't even imagine. What little I do know comes from those who have talked openly and honestly about their loss.

Nicholas Wolterstorff is one who has. In his book, *Lament for a Son,* he shared his feelings about the loss of his twenty-five-year-old son, Eric. Eric had entered college as a National Merit Scholar. He was bright and adventurous and had much to offer the world. Taking a break from working on his thesis, Eric had traveled to Austria. That is where the phone call came from one sunny Sunday afternoon.

> "Mr. Wolterstorff?"
> "Yes."
> "Is this Eric's father?"
> "Yes."

THE WEATHERING GRACE OF GOD

"Mr. Wolterstorff, I must give you some bad news."

"Yes."

"Eric has been climbing in the mountains and has had an accident."

"Yes."

"Eric has had a serious accident."

"Yes."

"Mr. Wolterstorff, I must tell you, Eric is dead. Mr. Wolterstorff, are you there? You must come at once! Mr. Wolterstoff, Eric is dead."

I have only one son. He is a nineteen-year-old, pre-med student who, like Eric, has much to offer the world. I cannot imagine *my* world without him. He calls from college, and just the sound of his voice brings me joy. He comes home from college, and just the sight of his smile makes me smile. What would it be like, I wonder, never to hear

THE TERRIFYING UPHEAVALS OF LIFE

that voice again, never to see that smile? I can't imagine. I couldn't bear it, I know that.

I don't know how my friends are bearing it.

Or Nicholas Wolterstorff.

Writing about it helps, I would think. Especially the painfully introspective way that Wolterstorff wrote about it.

It's the *neverness* that is so painful. *Never again* to be here with us—never to sit with us at table, never to travel with us, never to laugh with us, never to cry with us, never to embrace us as he leaves for school, never to see his brothers and sister marry. All the rest of our lives we must live without him. Only our death can stop the pain of his death.

A month, a year, five years—with that I could live. But not this forever.

I step outdoors into the moist moldy fragrance of an early summer morning and arm in arm with my

enjoyment comes the realization that never again will he smell this....

One small misstep and now this endless neverness.

After the shock of the tragic news came the pain. A cold, burning pain, as Wolterstorff described it. After the pain came the questions. "Why did he do it? Why did he climb that mountain? Why didn't he stay on flat earth? Why did he climb it alone? Why didn't he go with someone, roped up safely?"

The father knew the answers. He knew how much his son loved the mountains. That is why he climbed them. He knew his son preferred solitude to the company of strangers. That is why he climbed alone. He knew all those things. Even so, the questions kept coming. An avalanche of questions.

Wolterstorff writes:

THE TERRIFYING UPHEAVALS OF LIFE

I cannot fit it all together by saying, "He did it," but neither can I do so by saying, "There was nothing he could do about it." I cannot fit it together at all. I can only, with Job, endure. I do not know why God did not prevent Eric's death. To live without the answers is precarious. It's hard to keep one's footing.

Job's friends tried out on him their answer. "God did it, Job; he was the agent of your children's death. He did it because of some wickedness in you; he did it to punish you. Nothing indeed in your public life would seem to merit such retribution; it must then be something in your private inner life. Tell us what it is, Job. Confess."

The writer of Job refuses to say that God views the lives and deaths of children as cats-o'-nine-tails with which to lacerate parents.

I have no explanation. I can do nothing else than endure in the face of this deepest and most painful of

mysteries. I believe in God the Father Almighty, maker of heaven and earth and resurrecter of Jesus Christ. I also believe that my son's life was cut off in its prime. I cannot fit these pieces together. I am at a loss. I have read the theodices produced to justify the ways of God to man. I find them unconvincing. To the most agonized question I have ever asked I do not know the answer. I do not know why God would watch him fall.... I cannot even guess.

C.S. Lewis, writing about the death of his wife, was plainly angry with God. He, Lewis, deserved something better than to be treated so shabbily. I am not angry but baffled and hurt. My wound is an unanswered question. The wounds of all humanity are an unanswered question.

THE TERRIFYING UPHEAVALS OF LIFE

In times of upheaval, a voice from heaven says, "Be still and know that I am God."

It doesn't say, "Be still and know why."

In a distant day the gradual sacrament of understanding may be offered us.

Today what is offered us is the body and blood of Christ, who suffered, as George MacDonald once said, not that we might not suffer, but that our suffering might be like his.

His greatest suffering was the Cross.

Part of that suffering was an unanswered question.

From all those deadly, crushing, bitter experiences comes this delicate life and beauty, to teach us that what we in our faithless ignorance and fear call destruction is creation.

John Muir
"The Discovery of Glacier Bay"
Century Magazine, June 1895

THE WEATHERING
GRACE OF GOD

For the earth, the formation of its mountain ranges was a deadly, crushing, bitter experience. Irrepressible pressures crimped the stratified layers within the earth, pushing them through its surface. Massive shelves of rock shattered its crust. When the great lurchings subsided, the landscape lay rubbled with destruction.

Ages ago, glaciers covered the destruction we know as the Rocky Mountains, painstakingly sculpting them into the form they are today. Observing the glacial erosion in the Sierra Mountains, John Muir wrote:

Glaciers, back in their cold solitudes, work apart from men, exerting their tremendous energies in silence and darkness. Outspread, spirit-like, they brood above the predestined landscapes, work on

unwearied through immeasurable ages, until, in the fullness of time, the mountains and valleys are brought forth, channels furrowed for the rivers, basins made for the lakes and meadows, and long deep arms of the sea, soils spread for the forests and the fields.

Gradually the glaciers melted, unveiling a work in progress. Other forces went to work—the wind, the rain, and the slow erosion of the seasons. To this roughly quarried stone, the earth's weather was immediately drawn. Here is how the process worked and continues to work.

As the sun heats the earth, air expands and rises in columns called "thermals." That was one of the reasons why the Air Force Academy was located here on the Front Range. It is a perfect place to train young pilots. On any given day you can see them in their yellow gliders, riding these thermals, catching one column of air after another.

The higher these heated columns of air ascend, the more

they cool. The more they cool, the more they condense, forming a variety of cloud formations. The Front Range has an impressive, though ephemeral, collection of these formations. An armada of cumulus clouds in full sail. Broomswept wisps of cirrus clouds. And lenticular clouds, my favorite, hovering in the sky like softly rounded spaceships.

Added to this process, the warm, moist currents of the jet stream channel through the Rockies in a rushing river of wind. As the wind sloshes through the granite banks, the slopes shunt the wind upward, where it also cools and condenses, forming more clouds and churning up the wildest of weather.

Season after season, the weather transforms the landscape, chipping away at the jutting granite, washing away the crumbling limestone.

Winter snows come, melting when the temperature rises, sending water seeping into hairline fractures of granite. By night, the water freezes and expands, chiseling off bits

THE WEATHERING GRACE OF GOD

of gravel. Spring storms wash the gravel down the slopes. Melting snow feeds mountain streams, which, in turn, feed the flora and fauna.

In time, lichens attach themselves to rocks, small sponges of moss spring up, and soil begins to form. Windswept seeds of wild grasses sprout out of fissures. Birds and animals come, dropping other seeds from their fertilizing waste. The seeds grow into poppies, sumac bushes, Indian paintbrush. Seedling pines shoot up. Stands of aspen spread. Pine needles thatch the forest floor. Autumn's leaves crumble to mix with the rich layer of decay.

Slowly, imperceptibly, the weather softens the jagged edges of upheaval.

What once seemed to be destruction turns out to be creation. And out of these crushing experiences comes all this delicate life and beauty.

THE WEATHERING GRACE OF GOD

As mountains attract the weather, so the upheavals in our lives attract the grace of God. Those who have had deadly, crushing, bitter experiences happen to them are the ones to whom the Father is especially drawn.

The Lord is near to the brokenhearted.

PSALM 34:18

A broken and contrite heart, O God, Thou wilt not despise.

PSALM 51:17, KJV

He heals the brokenhearted, and binds up their wounds.

PSALM 147:3, NIV

Prophecies of the Messiah reveal that He, like the Father, would be drawn to those who have endured some devastating upheaval in their life.

THE WEATHERING GRACE OF GOD

The Spirit of the Lord God is upon me,
Because the Lord has anointed me—
To bring good news to the afflicted;
He has sent me to bind up the brokenhearted,
To proclaim liberty to captives,
And freedom to prisoners.

ISAIAH 61:1 (cf. Luke 4:18-19)

Behold My Servant, whom I uphold;
My chosen one in whom My soul delights.
I have put My Spirit upon Him;
He will bring forth justice to the nations.
He will not cry out or raise His voice,
Nor make His voice heard in the street.
A bruised reed He will not break,
And a dimly burning wick He will not extinguish.

ISAIAH 42:1-3 (cf. Matthew 12:18-21)

THE WEATHERING GRACE OF GOD

When the Messiah came, it was to the bruised reeds and dimly burning wicks of this world. It was to the sick, not the healthy. It was to the morally crippled, the mentally tormented, the physically afflicted, the relationally neglected. It was to those who had been devastated by some life-shattering loss. It was to a demon-possessed man who had lost his mind. To a woman at a well who had lost her reputation. To a leper who had lost his health. To a mother who had lost her son.

Here is the story of that mother.

Soon afterwards He went to a city called Nain; and His disciples were going along with Him, accompanied by a large crowd. Now as He approached the gate of the city, a dead man was being carried out, the only son of his mother, and she was a widow; and a sizeable crowd from the city was with her.

When the Lord saw her, He felt compassion for her,

and said to her, "Do not weep."

And He came up and touched the coffin; and the bearers came to a halt. And He said, "Young man, I say to you, arise!"

The dead man sat up, and began to speak. And Jesus gave him back to his mother. Fear gripped them all, and they began glorifying God, saying, "A great prophet has arisen among us!" and, "God has visited His people!"

LUKE 7:11-16

The miracle is an incredible display of the Savior's power. But there is something even more incredible about this auspicious meeting at the town gate.

This mother had not asked for a miracle. She had not thrown herself at the Savior's feet and begged for the life of her son. She hadn't demonstrated great faith. In fact, she hadn't demonstrated *any* faith at all. As far as

we know, she didn't even know who Jesus was.

Even so, He was drawn to her.

Her brokenness is what drew Him.

And what draws Him still.

At 8:31 A.M., May 18, 1980, Mount St. Helens reigned over the Washington state landscape as a benevolent monarch. At an elevation of 9,677 feet, it ruled over dense forests of Douglas fir and hemlock. North of the mountain, the calm surface of Spirit Lake reflected the majestic peak.

THE WEATHERING GRACE OF GOD

At 8:32, the monarch turned despot. In a moment of pent-up rage, Mount St. Helens erupted. The explosion had the force of twenty thousand atomic bombs the size of the one dropped on Hiroshima.

Within seconds the bulging north flank of the mountain slid away in the largest avalanche in United States history, triggering a lateral blast of hot gas, steam, and rock that shot across the landscape. An arm of the avalanche slammed nearby Spirit Lake, causing a tidal wave of destruction. Another arm threw a fourteen-mile punch down a river valley, sending the landscape reeling. The state of Washington staggered from the blow.

Plumes of ash billowed sixteen miles in the sky, blotting out the sun as it fanned out over Canada. Over the months ahead, the volcano continued to belch ash into the atmosphere that circled the world. In some places, deposits of ash, rock, and debris reached four hundred feet high.

THE WEATHERING GRACE OF GOD

The blast took 1,300 feet off the top of Mount St. Helens, destroying 150,000 acres of pristine wilderness. Entire forests were leveled, looking as if thousands of Pick-Up-Sticks had been suddenly dropped to the floor. The surface of nearby Spirit Lake was almost completely covered with trees that had been either sheared or uprooted by the blast. Over four billion board feet of lumber was damaged or destroyed, enough to build 150,000 homes.

The resulting landscape was lunar in its starkness. Geologists and forest officials believed it would be decades before the area would begin to recover.

In fact, the recovery began immediately.

When it was safe to visit the area, science fiction writer Ursala K. LeGuin came to survey the damage. In a poem titled "At Meta Lake: Autumn 1980," she described the emerging miracle that was taking place only a few months after the upheaval.

THE WEATHERING GRACE OF GOD

Thumb-high seedlings under blue shadow
  of May snow,
ignorant when the black blast came:
now they stand one here
  one there,
small green prayersticks,
feathers, powers,
in this steep dust encumbered
  with the dead.

Prayersticks. It's a beautiful image, isn't it? And a poignant one. For these are the prayers we pray after the black blast comes. Against all odds, they rise out of the dust. Small, but green. One here. One there. Thumb-high, but standing.

That is how the barrenness of our lives is reclaimed.

That is also how the barrenness around Mount St. Helens was reclaimed. After the blast, insects and rodents

emerged from their underground burrows, surveying the alien landscape. Gophers, moles, and mice tunneled through the ash, bringing soil to the surface. The wind blew seeds into these rodent holes, where they took root and grew. Sprigs of fireweed began dotting the land, followed by blooms of pink-flowered thistles, white-flowered lilies, and blue-flowered lupines.

Rain rinsed the ash from the land. Ferns and moss and mushrooms took root inside the fallen timber. Spiders staked their claims with webbed determination. Bluebirds returned to the area, looking for easy prey. Other birds returned, building nests inside the upright remains of splintered trees.

Huckleberries and thimbleberries tufted through the soil, bringing foraging animals. Elk were among the first of the larger animals to return. As they wandered over the moonscape, they left tracks into which windswept seeds collected and sprouted. First to grow were deciduous

trees, the cottonwood and alder. Later came the ever-greens, the fir and hemlock.

The area has a long way to go to become beautiful. But the beginnings of beauty are everywhere. And where there were prayersticks, now there are trees.

▼▲▼▲▼

In his book, *The Man Who Planted Trees*, Jean Giono tells of his encounter with a shepherd in the French Alps, named Elzeard Bouffler. At the time, because of careless deforestation, the mountains around Provence, France, were barren. Former villages were deserted because their springs and brooks had run dry. The wind blew furiously, unimpeded by foliage.

THE WEATHERING GRACE OF GOD

While mountain climbing, Giono came to a shepherd's hut, where he was invited to spend the night.

After dinner Giono watched the shepherd meticulously sort through a pile of acorns, discarding those that were cracked or undersized. When the shepherd had counted out one hundred perfect acorns, he stopped for the night and went to bed.

Giono learned that the fifty-five-year-old shepherd had been planting trees on the wild hillsides for over three years. He had planted 100,000 trees, 20,000 of which had sprouted. Of those, he expected half to be eaten by rodents or die due to the elements, and the other half to live.

After World War I, Giono returned to the mountainside and discovered incredible rehabilitation: there was a veritable forest, accompanied by a chain reaction in nature. Water flowed in the once-empty brooks. The ecology, sheltered by a leafy roof and bonded to the earth by a mat of spreading roots, became hospitable. Willows, rushes,

meadows, gardens, and flowers were birthed.

Giono returned again after World War II. Twenty miles from the lines, the shepherd had continued his work, ignoring the war of 1939, just as he had ignored that of 1914. The reclamation of the land continued. Whole regions glowed with health and prosperity.

Giono writes: "On the site of the ruins I had seen in 1913 now stand neat farms.... The old streams, fed by the rains and snows that the forest conserves, are flowing again.... Little by little, the villages have been rebuilt. People from the plains, where land is costly, have settled here, bringing youth, motion, the spirit of adventure."

THE WEATHERING GRACE OF GOD

The barren mountains around Provence, France, were reclaimed a seed at a time. It took years to sow them, and years to grow them. Little by little life returned. First the trees. Then the streams. And finally the villages, teeming with new life and the spirit of adventure.

When upheavals deforest the landscape of our lives, the streams and brooks of our spiritual life often dry up. Unimpeded by foliage, emotional winds blow over us furiously, winds similar to those recorded in John Steinbeck's novel, *The Grapes of Wrath*.

Steinbeck's novel tells the story of the great exodus of farmers who left Oklahoma to make a new start for themselves in California. The story focuses on the pilgrimage of one particular family named the Joads. Their family, along with so many others, had endured not only the ravages of the Great Depression but the winds of the Dust Bowl. These unrelenting winds swept the topsoil from their farms. With the loss of the soil came the loss of their crops.

THE WEATHERING GRACE OF GOD

With the loss of their crops came the loss of their livelihood. With the loss of their livelihood came the loss of their farms.

In the opening chapter, Steinbeck describes these winds and the devastation they brought with them.

A day went by and the wind increased, steady, unbroken by gusts. The dust from the roads fluffed up and spread out and fell on the weeds beside the fields.... Little by little the sky was darkened by the mixing dust, and the wind felt over the earth, loosened the dust, and carried it away. The wind grew stronger.... The corn threshed in the wind and made a dry, rushing sound. The finest dust did not settle back to earth now, but disappeared into the darkening sky.

The wind grew stronger, whisked under stones, carried up straws and old leaves, and even little clods, marking its course as it sailed across the fields. The

THE WEATHERING GRACE OF GOD

air and the sky darkened and through them the sun shone redly, and there was a raw sting in the air. During the night the wind raced faster over the land, dug cunningly among the rootlets of corn, and the corn fought the wind with its weakened leaves until the roots were freed by the prying wind and then each stalk settled wearily sideways toward the earth and pointed the direction of the wind.

The dawn came, but no day. In the gray sky a red sun appeared, a dim red circle that gave a little light, like dusk; and as that day advanced, the dusk slipped back toward darkness, and the wind cried and whimpered over the fallen corn.

Men and women huddled in their houses, and they tied handkerchiefs over their noses when they went out, and wore goggles to protect the eyes.

When the night came again it was a black night, for the stars could not pierce the dust to get down,

THE WEATHERING GRACE OF GOD

and the window lights could not even spread beyond their own yards. Now the dust was evenly mixed with the air, an emulsion of dust and air. Houses were shut tight, and cloth wedged around doors and windows, but the dust came so thinly that it could not be seen in the air, and it settled like pollen on the chairs and tables, on the dishes.

An upheaval not only alters the landscape but often deforests the landscape, leading to further devastation. The same thing can happen when tragedy strikes the small, forty-acre farm that is our life.

Steinbeck's description of the Dust Bowl is what the weather of the heart is sometimes like for someone who has endured a great loss. A steady wind blows over you, opposes you, oppresses you. The wind grows stronger, whisking away what little soil surrounds the few rootlets of spiritual life you have left. With the wind comes sting-

ing reminders of how different your life is from everyone else's. Other people talk together, shop together, dine together, laugh together. And the taken-for-granted normalness of their lives stings your face so raw you can't bear it. Your bloodshot eyes burn from the windblown grit. Your tears wash away the grit, but not the burn.

To escape these stinging realities, you huddle yourself in your house. You wedge cloth around the doors and windows, anything to shut out the outside world. But a thin layer of dust covers everything. No matter how thorough you are in your dusting, there is always something you have overlooked, always some reminder of your loss.

You lie in bed at night, staring at the ceiling. Your thoughts are incoherent pieces of a puzzle you have grown weary of, yet can't get rid of. The headache won't go away. Or the guilt. Or the regret. You're out of tears, out of prayers. You've waited in silence, wept in silence, wondered in silence. You wonder if anyone is up there, beyond that ceiling, if anyone was *ever* up there, or if it has all

THE WEATHERING GRACE OF GOD

been just so much pious talk and positive thinking, reinforced by the peer pressure of your religious friends.

Outside the sky is darkened. The night is black. Light from heaven, once as sparkling as a star-studded sky, cannot pierce the airborne dust. What little light you have within you doesn't spread very far, either.

Through the night the wind continues. The night is long and it seems the dawn will never come. Finally the dawn comes, but no day. A gray sky veils the sun. And God, who once seemed so radiant, now seems a dim red circle that gives little light.

Eventually the wind subsides, the dust settles, and it is safe to go outside again. What then? How do we reclaim the Dust Bowl that our life has become? Where do we even start?

We start by realizing that reclaiming the land doesn't happen overnight. It didn't happen overnight in Provence. It didn't happen overnight in Oklahoma. And it doesn't happen overnight in the wind-stripped terrain of our own lives.

THE WEATHERING GRACE OF GOD

But it *does* happen. And it begins to happen when we pray. Each time we pray, we plant a seed. It takes years to sow them. Even more years to grow them. That is how we cooperate with God in reclaiming the landscape. A seed at a time. We plant them in faith, not knowing how many will sprout, or of those that sprout, how many will survive. And though the odds are against us, we believe that some of those seeds *will* take root, that some of them *will* survive, and that someday they *will* make a difference in the landscape of our lives.

Yet there are days when the promise of "someday" is not enough. You try to think of a reason to go on living *today*. But today you can't. And from your trembling hand, the only seed you have to sow is the prayer that God in His mercy will put an end to your misery, and take you home. Not someday but today.

THE WEATHERING GRACE OF GOD

How do we sort through the pile of **acorns** that is our words, when they are either cracked or undersized? And if those are the only words on our table, dare we sow them?

The language of prayer spans the lexicon of human emotion. There are the light vowels of joy and the low gutturals of sorrow. There are the gliding consonants of faith and the hard consonants of doubt. The syntax is sometimes clear, other times convoluted. The sentences are sometimes punctuated with exclamation marks, other times with question marks.

This is as it should be, if it is to be an honest dialogue. C.S. Lewis said that "we should to bring to God what is in us, not what ought to be in us." The "oughts" will keep us from telling the truth. They will also keep us from feeling the truth. Especially the truth about our pain.

We can be too careful with our words, especially when we pray. We can be too quick to come to conclusions

THE WEATHERING GRACE OF GOD

about what happened to us and why. Too quick to make sense of it all. Too quick to see God in it all.

When Jesus received news of John the Baptist's death, He didn't draw a lesson from it, didn't talk about what good might come from it. He went away by Himself and mourned (Matthew 14:1-13).

When Jesus realized the nearness of His own death, He went to a quiet place and prayed (Matthew 26:36-46). Into that garden, where the shadows of death surrounded Him, Jesus brought His closest friends. His soul, He told them, was "deeply grieved, to the point of death" (Matthew 26:38). He wanted them there, needed them there. Desperately.

Jesus reached into the depths of His soul for whatever words He could find that spoke the truth of His pain. Many of those words cut Him on their way up. We are told that He agonized with "loud crying and tears" (Hebrews 5:7). We are also told that He fell to the ground, where

THE WEATHERING GRACE OF GOD

He prayed fervently and sweated profusely (Luke 22:44).

This was no Renaissance painting. This was a real portrait, a portrait of how we pray when the earth beneath our feet begins to quake. We pray however we can, with whatever words we can. We pray with our sweat, with our tears. And with whatever friends we have who will sit with us in the darkness.

THE WEATHERING GRACE OF GOD

Gethsemane. Calvary. And any other place in the world where tears are wept but unblotted, where questions are asked but unanswered. A place like Bosnia or Somalia or Auschwitz.

Holocaust survivor Elie Wiesel was thirteen years old when he entered Auschwitz. By the time he left there, he had lost his entire family and witnessed unspeakable horrors. He did not speak of the horrors until ten years later when he wrote the book, *Night*.

Before being sent to the camps, Elie was a devout Jew. To mentor him, he sought out a religious master, named Moshe. Here is what Moshe taught him about prayer.

"Why do you weep when you pray?" he asked me, as though he had known me a long time.

"I don't know why," I answered, greatly disturbed.

THE WEATHERING GRACE OF GOD

The question had never entered my head. I wept because—because of something inside me that felt the need for tears. That was all I knew.

Why did I pray? A strange question. Why did I live? Why did I breathe?

"I don't know why," I said, even more disturbed and ill at ease. "I don't know why."

After that day I saw him often. He explained to me with great insistence that every question possessed a power that did not lie in the answer.

"Man raises himself toward God by the questions he asks Him," he was fond of repeating. "That is the true dialogue. Man questions God and God answers. But we don't understand His answers. We can't understand them. Because they come from the depths of the soul, and they stay there until death. You will find the true answers, Eliezer, only within yourself!"

"And why do you pray, Moshe?" I asked him.

THE WEATHERING GRACE OF GOD

"I pray to the God within me that He will give me the strength to ask Him the right questions."

Who of us knows what those questions are? Or how deeply within ourselves we will have to go to find them? Who knows what we will find in those depths?

Maybe something of the secret of who we are.

Who we are, who we *truly* are, is a secret known only to God. One day we will be given the stone that bears our new name (Revelation 2:17). But today, that name is a mystery, even to us.

Mystery is an unsettling concept, especially for those of us who are Protestants. Protestants have no place for mystery. If there is, it is a small place, and one we feel confident that can be explained in time, given enough scrutiny.

Catholics are much better at this, I think. Mystery is something they not only make a place for, but kneel before. Unlike them, Protestants have an almost

obsessive-compulsive need for clarity, which is not so much a theological need as it is a psychological one. I think we feel if we can somehow connect all the dots in life in some kind of cause-and-effect manner that life can be managed and made safe for us and for those we love.

But the universe cannot be managed or made safe. Not by us anyway. When we lose a sense of mystery, we lose a sense of our place in the universe. And leaving that place, we leave behind a humility that is attendant to that place.

Mystery, ambiguity, uncertainty. These are places where we reach an end of ourselves, places where we have to stop, stop and take off our shoes. If we don't, the mystery, the ambiguity, the uncertainty will one day prove too much for us. If we must have all our questions answered before we can go forward in our relationship with God, there will come a day when we won't go forward. It may come at Gethsemane. At Calvary. Or Auschwitz.

Or at the death of a son.

Or at the death of a friend's son.

THE WEATHERING GRACE OF GOD

Who knows what day that one question will go unanswered?

All we know is that one day it will. It did for Jesus. And it will for us.

In the meantime, we are surrounded by mystery. Who we are is a mystery. What role we play in the unfolding drama of redemption is also a mystery. How long we will play that role is a mystery, too. Some mysteries remain God's secrets. Others Jesus shares with us, the way He shared with Peter something of the secret of His own life.

"Truly, truly, I say to you, when you were younger, you used to gird yourself, and walk wherever you wished; but when you grow old, you will stretch out your hands, and someone else will gird you, and bring you where you do not wish to go."

Now this He said, signifying by what kind of death He would glorify God.

JOHN 21:18-19

THE WEATHERING GRACE OF GOD

Our lives are part of an over-arching drama, part sunshine, part rain, that spans the heavens from Paradise to Paradise. What role we play in that drama is a secret Jesus shares with us, if at all, at His own discretion. The most personal secrets of our story are seldom shared with anyone else. The continuation of Jesus' conversation with Peter is a case in point.

> Peter, turning around, saw the disciple whom Jesus loved, following them; the one who also had leaned back on His bosom at the supper, and said, "Lord, who is the one who betrays you?"
> Jesus said to him, "If I want him to remain until I come, what is that to you? You follow Me!"
>
> JOHN 21:20-22

The secret of my friends' story is a mystery. It is not mine to know. It may not even be theirs to know, not now

anyway. For now we see in a glass darkly, but then face to face, and now we know in part, but then we shall know fully just as we have been fully known (1 Corinthians 13:12).

So until then, what?

We feel our way in the dark.

Until we find each other.

We huddle together in the storm.

Wet and shivering, but together.

And maybe in the end it will be our huddling in the storm that gives us more comfort than our understanding of the storm.

THE WEATHERING GRACE OF GOD

In a letter to a young poet, dated July 16, 1903, the German poet, Rainer Maria Rilke wrote:

> Be patient toward all that is unsolved in your heart and try to love the *questions themselves* like locked rooms and like books that are written in a very foreign tongue. Do not now seek the answers, which cannot be given you because you would not be able to live them. And the point is, to live everything. *Live* the questions now. Perhaps you will then gradually, without noticing it, live along some distant day into the answer.

God doesn't ask us to figure out our salvation, with confidence and certainty. He asks us to *work* it out, with fear and trembling (Philippians 2:12). Living the questions is part of the way we do that. It is an honest way. It is also a

painful way. The Scriptures help, but not with the pain. The Scriptures are not a medicine cabinet, filled with prescriptions to take the edge off of life. They are about a God who, during His most painful experience on earth, refused the wine mixed with myrrh that was offered Him.

The Scriptures show us what life with such a God is like.

My God, my God, why have You forsaken me? Why are You so far from saving me, so far from the words of my groaning?

PSALM 22:1, NIV

Why, O Lord, do You stand far off? Why do You hide Yourself in times of trouble?

PSALM 10:1, NIV

THE WEATHERING GRACE OF GOD

What gain is there in my destruction, in my going down to the pit? Will the dust praise You? Will it proclaim Your faithfulness?

PSALM 30:9, NIV

How long, O Lord? Will You forget me forever? How long will You hide Your face from me?

PSALM 13:1, NIV

Why must I go about mourning, oppressed by the enemy?

PSALM 42:9, NIV

How long must I wrestle with my thoughts and every day have sorrow in my heart?

PSALM 13:2, NIV

THE WEATHERING GRACE OF GOD

Painful questions, all of them. Unanswered questions, many of them. And we, if we live long enough and honestly enough, one dark day we will ask them, too.

For two disciples, Christ's crucifixion was an upheaval so great that the landscape in Jerusalem, where it happened, was too grim a reminder of their pain. To sift through the emotional rubble, they had to get away. The road they took was the road to Emmaus, a village seven miles away.

At some time or another we have all taken that road, or else at sometime or another we will. The road these disciples traveled sloped away from Jerusalem through desolate and uncertain terrain, a stark reflection of the desolation and uncertainty within them. The Savior they so loved had been brutally killed. With Him died their hopes, their dreams, their futures. Something of themselves died, too. And something of their faith. Who knows what sorrow

they carried with them on that road out of town, what they talked about, what they cried about, what they feared would happen next? Who knows what questions they asked or what emotions surfaced when they asked them?

Gradually, over that seven-mile stretch of road, the answer to their questions became clear. It happened like this. As they walked away, Jesus came alongside them, walked with them, and engaged them in a dialogue about what had happened. At first, they didn't recognize Him. They came to the outskirts of Emmaus, and still they didn't recognize Him. It wasn't until they sat down to dine with Him, and He with them, that their eyes were finally opened, both to the identity of God's Son and to the mystery of God's ways.

The story illustrates what Rilke meant when he advised that young poet to "live the questions." He meant that we should take the questions with us wherever we go. "The point is, to live everything." Everything that happens to us

should be brought into a dialogue with God, an honest and ongoing dialogue. No experience should be excluded. No question should be, either. "*Live* the questions now," Rilke advised. "Perhaps you will then gradually, without noticing it, live along some distant day into the answer."

The answer may come in a seven-mile walk.

Or in a walk that lasts a lifetime.

It may never come.

And yet we go on asking, seeking, knocking.

One wonders why.

Our unanswered questions are the grappling hooks we use to scale the North Face of God, who seems at times an Everest of indifference. The ascent is treacherous. And maybe why we brave the climb is because we sense that abandoning the climb might be even more treacherous.

One learns that the world, though made, is yet being made. That this is still the morning of creation. That mountains, long conceived, are now being born, brought to light by the glaciers, channels traced for rivers, basins hollowed for lakes. That moraine soil is being ground and outspread for coming plants ... while the finest part of the grist, seen hastening far out to sea, is being stored away in the darkness, and builded, particle on particle, cementing and crystalizing, to make mountains and valleys, and plains of other land-scapes, and pass on through the ages in endless rhythm and beauty.

John Muir
"Alaska Glaciers"
San Francisco Daily Evening Bulletin
September 27, 1879

THE CONTINUING
LANDSCAPE OF FAITH

In an article titled, *My First Summer in the Sierra* (September 2, 1869), John Muir wrote:

One is constantly reminded of the infinite lavishness and fertility of Nature—inexhaustible abundance amid what seems enormous waste. And yet when we look into any of her operations that lie within reach of our minds, we learn that no particle of her material is wasted or worn out. It is eternally flowing from use to use, beauty to yet higher beauty; and we soon cease to lament waste and death, and rather rejoice and exult in the imperishable, unspendable wealth of the universe, and faithfully watch and wait the reappearance of everything that melts and fades and dies about us, feeling sure that its next appearance will be better and more beautiful than the last.

THE WEATHERING GRACE OF GOD

If there truly are seasons of our life that correspond to seasons of the earth, and if we live, say, eighty years, then each season spans twenty of them. Which raises a question. If spring is the first twenty years of our life and winter the last twenty, what season does that put us in, you and me?

For me, it's autumn. More precisely, October. More precisely still, mid-October. For years now I've been passing myself off as middle-aged, which, when I do the math, I discover is a lie.

I have lived the past eight years of my life in Colorado. I have loved every day, especially the days of autumn, which is my favorite time of the year. It is a season conducive to reflection, and that is one of the reasons I love it.

Signs of the changing season are everywhere. Birds have migrated. Other animals have hibernated. And insects have gone wherever it is that insects go. The grass has stopped growing. The leaves have started falling. A few tardy chipmunks scurry over the forest floor foraging for a final meal before they cozy into their burrows.

Signs of a changing season are everywhere with me as

well. When I look at my hands, the skin is not as supple as it once was, the grip not as strong. When I look in the mirror, I see changes there, too. The color of my hair over the years has weathered from red to chestnut to a tired brown that is graying around the temples. Like autumn's thinning leaves, my hair is thinning, too.

"In October, when the leaves fall, you can see deeper into the forest."

The words are Richard Seltzer's from his book, *Letters to a Young Doctor.* They make me think of the many leaves that have fallen from my life. Grandparents, on both sides of the family. A father to heart disease. An aunt to Alzheimer's. A friend to a heart attack. Another friend to cancer. Another to AIDS. The son of a friend to suicide.

Leaves are falling from my body, too. A knee to a football injury. A back to ruptured disks. My hearing. My sight. My memory. None of those are gone. Even so, I feel a nip in the autumn air, and I know that winter is on its

way, chillingly insensitive to how unprepared I am for its coming.

Other leaves have fallen, too. Other losses line the forest floor. The loss of one child to motherhood, three other children to college. The loss of who I once thought myself to be to who I now know myself to be. The loss of certainty in my relationship with God.

Everything around us, said Muir, "melts and fades and dies." And yet, he contends, "no material is wasted or worn out."

But if it isn't wasted and worn out, what happens to it?

It reappears.

The hope of nature is that the "next appearance will be better and more beautiful than the last."

THE CONTINUING LANDSCAPE OF FAITH

I notice a brittle colony of leaves huddled against the winter chill. Seeing them reminds me of the fact that life grows out of the life that went before it. Sometimes I forget that. It is the losses of autumn that bring the gains of spring.

Other losses bring other gains. The loss of a child to motherhood brings the gain of grandchildren. The loss of children to college brings the gain of their emergence as adults. The loss of hearing brings the gain in appreciation of voices that are dear to me, voices I one day may no longer be able to hear. The loss of illusions about myself is a gain in understanding of who I am, who we all are, and how much each of us needs to be understood, loved, forgiven. And how much we, in turn, need to understand one another, love one another, forgive one another. The loss of certainty in my relationship with God, with all its questions and confusion and tears, is a gain of honesty in that relationship.

THE WEATHERING GRACE OF GOD

It has been painful to learn, but I have learned that with every loss comes a gain, if nothing more than the compassion we feel for others who have suffered similar losses.

Gain comes out of loss the way life grows out of the life that went before it. My son grew out of me as his son will one day grow out of him. I think of those things as I walk the reservoir with him. He walks beside me and slightly ahead of me. He could easily run the reservoir, but he walks, shortening his stride so as not to outdistance me.

I sometimes think of my father when I see my son. He died when my son was four. My son remembers his grandfather, but in time the memories will fade. Even so, there are some things that won't fade. Something of my dad lives on in him. Some of it is genetic. He has my father's smile, and his dimples. His feet, too.

He is artistic. Some of that comes from me, some from his mother. And farther back, from my mother and my wife's father. He is kind and sensitive and giving. Some of

THE CONTINUING LANDSCAPE OF FAITH

that is from us, too. I am beginning to realize, though, that much of who he is did not originate with us. It merely passed through us. There seems to be some kind of spiritual DNA that assembles itself differently in each generation. Traits that might be recessive in one generation recombine to become dominant in another.

A big part of his spiritual DNA has been constructed by prayer. Some of that comes from his mother and me. Some of it goes farther back. My mother has faithfully prayed for her three children, seven grandchildren, and two great-grandchildren. And before her, her mother. And before her mother, who knows how many generations have contributed to who he is, "eternally flowing from use to use, beauty to yet higher beauty"? My mother-in-law prays for all of us, too. And who knows how far back those genes go?

The seasons come and go, generation after generation. The gains of spring come from all that is lost in the fall.

Life grows out of the life that went before it. As everything that makes me who I am begins to melt and fade and die, I am not disheartened by the losses. I see my son walking beside me and slightly ahead of me, and I am filled with hope, "feeling sure that its next appearance will be better and more beautiful than the last."

e makes everything beautiful in its time." The words are Solomon's (Eccesiastes. 3:11). The "He" is God. The Hebrew word for "beautiful" is *yapheh*. It is the same word used in Genesis 12 to describe Sarah.

THE CONTINUING LANDSCAPE OF FAITH

Now there was a famine in the land; so Abram went down to Egypt to sojourn there, for the famine was severe in the land.

It came about when he came near to Egypt, that he said to Sarai his wife, "See now, I know that you are a *beautiful* woman; and when the Egyptians see you, they will say, 'This is his wife'; and they will kill me, but they will let you live. Please say that you are my sister so that it may go well with me because of you, and that I may live on account of you."

It came about when Abram came into Egypt, the Egyptians saw that the woman was very *beautiful*. Pharaoh's officials saw her and praised her to Pharaoh; and the woman was taken into Pharaoh's house. Therefore he treated Abram well for her sake; and gave him sheep and oxen and donkeys and male and female servants and female donkeys and camels.

(vv. 10-16, italics mine)

Sarah was not just beautiful, she was stunningly beautiful. Everywhere she went, heads turned.

God's purpose is to make *us* beautiful. How beautiful? *Stunningly* beautiful. As beautiful as His Son in all His glory (Romans 8:18-19, 29-30).

Augustine was so captivated by the beauty of Christ that he composed a song about it:

> He is beautiful in heaven, beautiful on earth; beautiful in the womb, beautiful in his parents' arms, beautiful in his miracles, beautiful in inviting to life, beautiful in not worrying about death, beautiful in giving his life and beautiful in taking it up again; he is beautiful on the cross, beautiful in the tomb, beautiful in heaven. Listen to the song with understanding, and let not the weakness of the flesh distract your eyes from the splendor of his beauty.

THE CONTINUING LANDSCAPE OF FAITH

There is much in this world to distract us from the splendor of Christ's beauty. There is much in the Church to distract us. And much within ourselves. There is so much ugliness in the world, and that is what sometimes distracts us. There is ugliness in the Church, too. And within ourselves.

But there is no ugliness in Jesus. He is altogether beautiful. Someday the beauty that is His will be ours. For it has not yet appeared what we shall be like, but when Jesus appears, we shall see Him as He is. And seeing Him, we shall become like Him (1 John 3:2).

THE WEATHERING GRACE OF GOD

Until we see Him in heaven, we must live out our lives east of Eden, in a land of thorned resistance. We seek life's ease, but ease is not a gift this life has to offer. The life we have been given is lived by the strain of our back and the sweat of our brow.

The contrast between eastern and western Colorado illustrates the difference between life as we want it and life as we are given it. But it illustrates something else—the difference between the life of David and his son Solomon.

Solomon, whose name literally means, "peaceful one," ruled Israel in an unprecedented reign of peace. He lived a life of privilege, studying, writing, hosting elaborate parties, collecting the most exquisite art, listening to the finest music, breeding the best animals, building dream houses and meticulously landscaping them (Ecclesiastes 2:1-10).

Solomon's life was smooth and predictable.

THE CONTINUING LANDSCAPE OF FAITH

It was eastern Colorado.

David's life was ridged with upheavals.

It was western Colorado.

Where they lived their lives, I believe, had much to do with how they ended their lives. The epitaph of David's life was that he was a man after God's own heart (Acts 13:22). The epitaph of Solomon's life was that his heart was not totally devoted to the Lord as his father David's had been (1 Kings 11:4).

Which makes me wonder. How would I want *my* obituary to read? What would I want chiseled onto *my* tombstone? How would *I* want to be remembered?

I would want to be remembered the way David was remembered. Who of us wouldn't? But then, who of us would want the life that led to such an epitaph?

I want David's epitaph, but I want Solomon's life. That's the rub.

Solomon was a wise man and a preacher. David was a

warrior and a poet. Although Solomon wrote songs (1 Kings 4:32, Song of Solomon), he is perhaps best known for his teaching (Proverbs) and his preaching (Ecclesiastes). David, on the other hand, is best known for his song-writing (Psalms). So many of his psalms were written after major upheavals in his life. The superscriptions introducing each psalm give the context of the upheaval.

Psalm 3, for example, is "A Psalm of David, when he fled from Absalom his son."

Psalm 18, "A Psalm of David the servant of the Lord, who spoke to the Lord the words of this song in the day that the Lord delivered him from the hand of all his enemies and from the hand of Saul."

Psalm 34, "A Psalm of David when he feigned madness before Abimelech, who drove him away and he departed."

Psalm 51, "A Psalm of David, when Nathan the prophet came to him after he had gone in to Bathsheba."

Psalm 52, "A Maskil of David, when Doeg the Edomite

THE CONTINUING LANDSCAPE OF FAITH

came and told Saul, and he said to him, 'David has come to the house of Abimelech.'"

Psalm 54, "A Maskil of David, when the Ziphites came and said to Saul, 'Is not David hiding himself among us?'"

Psalm 56, "A Miktham of David, when the Philistines seized him at Gath."

Psalm 57, "A Miktham of David, when he fled from Saul, in the cave."

Psalm 59, "A Miktham of David, when Saul sent men, and they watched the house in order to kill him."

Psalm 60, "A Miktham of David, to teach; when he struggled with Aram-naharaim and with Aram-zobah, and Joab returned, and smote twelve thousand of Edom in the valley of Salt."

Psalm 63, "A Psalm of David, when he was in the wilderness of Judah."

Psalm 142, "A Maskil of David, when he was in a cave. A prayer."

THE WEATHERING GRACE OF GOD

The life of faith is a Lewis-and-Clark expedition into uncharted territory. The book of Psalms maps that territory with exacting honesty. Much of that map belongs to David. The landscape of his life was a vast range of upheavals. Three of the peaks stand out against the horizon of biblical history. His relationship with Saul. His relationship with Absalom. And his relationship with Bathsheba.

His relationship with Saul turned out to be one that was filled with great pain (1 Samuel 24).

The relationship with his son Absalom caused him even greater grief (2 Samuel 15:12-17). Can you imagine what it would be like to have your own flesh and blood rebel against you, divide the military against you, and plot to kill you?

Then there was David's relationship with Bathsheba. While his troops were off to battle, he took the wife of one of his most loyal warriors, had sex with her, then sent

orders to the front lines to have her husband killed (2 Samuel 11).

His relationship with Saul was an upheaval he was in no way responsible for. His conduct was above reproach. Though unjustly persecuted, David never retaliated.

Not much is revealed about David's relationship with Absalom. Most of the failure in the relationship can be placed squarely on Absalom's shoulders. But maybe David shared some of it. Maybe he wasn't the father to him that he could have been. Maybe Absalom felt abandoned and his abandonment turned to aggression. Who knows? We are not told.

David's relationship with Bathsheba, on the other hand, was all *his* doing. He initiated the sexual encounter, had her husband Uriah murdered, and tried to cover it all up with lies and deception. The upheaval nearly destroyed him. At best, it could have cost him his job. At worst, his life. Yet God, in His mercy, spared him both conse-

quences. He did, however, exact other consequences, painful consequences he would have to live with the rest of his life (2 Samuel 12:7-15).

Of all the upheavals in David's life, this was Pike's Peak. This was the one failure that would dominate the landscape of his life. It would be named. It would be seen by everyone and remembered by everyone. Forever.

If God truly does make all things beautiful in its time, what possible beauty could He bring from this?

It took a thousand years, but the beauty finally came. It is recorded in the first chapter of Matthew. We can see it by starting at the first verse, then skipping down to the sixth.

The book of the genealogy of Jesus Christ, the son of David... (v. 1).

And to David was born Solomon by her who had been the wife of Uriah (v. 6).

Through the union of David and Bathsheba came the Savior of the world. For all the consequences of David's sin that we could name, could any of us have ever named that one? In our wildest imagination, who of us could have foreseen such beauty coming from such ugliness?

The word for it is *grace*.

It is who God is. It is what He does.

He makes everything beautiful in its time.

Everything.

He may take a lifetime to do it. He may take a lineage of lifetimes. But in its time, He makes everything beautiful.

Even the ugliest of David's sins.

Even the ugliest of ours.

THE WEATHERING GRACE OF GOD

There are moments when I have been overwhelmed by all the ugliness in the world. The hatred. The violence. The prejudice. The injustice. The cruelty. You don't have to flip through the channels very long to see it. Newsreel footage of the Holocaust. Horror stories from the here and now. Gangs in the inner city. Drugs in the suburbs. AIDS in sub-Saharan Africa. Starvation in India. Rapes on college campuses. Kidnappings. Murders. Drive-by shootings.

The state flower of Colorado is the columbine. That should remind us of all the beauty in the world. When we hear it, though, we don't think of a flower. We think of a high school and the terror that happened there.

So much ugliness. So much pain. It is overwhelming sometimes.

It overwhelmed John Coffey. Coffey is the central character in the movie, *The Green Mile*. The story is set in death row of a southern prison in the 1930s. John Coffey is a large, black man who has been wrongly convicted of a

brutal crime. As the guards discover, the man has the miraculous power to heal. He also has a prophetic gifting that allows him to see crimes that have been committed. Just by touching the arm of one of the death-row inmates, for example, he sees the horrible rapes and murders that this man has committed.

Paul, the head guard, played by Tom Hanks, comes to realize that John Coffey is innocent. He asks John if he wants him to fight to get him off death row. The weeping John Coffey declines the offer, explaining: "I's tired, boss. Tired of bein' on the road, lonely as a sparrow in the rain. Tired of not ever having me a buddy to be with, or tell me where we's coming from or going to, or why. Mostly I'm tired of people being ugly to each other. I'm tired of all the pain I feel and hear in the world every day. There's too much of it. It's like pieces of glass in my head all the time. Can you understand?"

I can. My guess is that you can, too.

THE WEATHERING GRACE OF GOD

There are times when all the ugliness in the world overwhelms us. There are other times, though, when a moment bursts, and we are drenched with so much beauty that it rinses us of such thoughts. Such a moment takes place in the movie *American Beauty*.

One of the subplots of the movie involves a relationship that develops between a teenage girl and a boy who has moved in next door. Initially, the girl is antagonistic toward him because he is quiet and quirky. One of his quirks is that he takes a video camera with him everywhere he goes, filming sometimes the most unusual things. The girl, somewhat of an outsider herself, becomes increasingly drawn to him, and a relationship develops.

The boy invites her into his house, asking if she wants to see the most beautiful thing he has ever filmed. She says yes, and he puts a videotape into the big-screen TV. They sit in the darkened room, their eyes fixed to the screen where a small funnel of wind is swirling around a

tattered bunch of autumn leaves. Caught in the vortex is a crumbled, white, plastic bag. The boy describes the setting. "It was one of those days when it's a minute away from snowing ... and there was this electricity in the air. You can almost hear it. And this bag was dancing with me ... like a little kid, begging me to play with it ... for fifteen minutes. That's the day I realized there was this entire life behind things. And this incredibly benevolent force who wanted me to know that there was no reason to be afraid. Ever. Maybe that was a poor excuse, I know. But it helps me remember. I need to remember."

The camera no longer focuses on the TV screen but on the boy's face. His eyes glisten with emotion as he watches the plastic bag twirling in the air. His lips quiver as he continues, pausing between the phrases. "Sometimes there is ... so much beauty in the world ... I feel I can't take it. And my heart ... is just going to ... cave in."

It was a beautiful moment. It touched me because I

have had moments like that myself, as I'm sure you have had as well. Moments when you feel you have touched the hem of some divine garment, and you sense a healing power flowing into you. The moments are so tangible you almost expect to hear a voice respond by asking, "Who touched me?"

C.S. Lewis talked about such moments in his sermon, "The Weight of Glory." He talked about the universal longings we have for beauty. He believed that, of all people, poets and writers of mythology understood this longing best. "We do not merely want to *see* beauty, though, God knows, even that is bounty enough," he wrote. "We want something else which can hardly be put into words—to be united with the beauty we see, to pass into it, to receive it into ourselves, to bathe in it, to become part of it."

That is what I think the boy experienced when he saw the plastic bag twirling about in the air. The image stirred within him the longing to be united with the beauty he saw. To enter the ballroom and join in the dance.

"At present," Lewis continues, "we are on the outside of the world, the wrong side of the door. We cannot mingle with the splendours we see. But all the leaves of the New Testament are rustling with the rumour that it will not always be so. Some day, God willing, we shall get *in*."

I have had moments when it seemed I was at the railing that separates heaven and earth, and there was offered a sacrament. The sacrament may have been some hauntingly beautiful music or the echo of an elk bugling in the mountains. It may have been a freshly-cut-peach sunset or a crayoned work of refrigerator art. It may have been a verse of Scripture or a line from Shakespeare.

Whatever your moments have been, you sensed that something sacred was being offered you. Receiving them, you knew somehow, and with great certainty, that this was not your home, that your home was the place where

your deepest longings were leading you, somewhere beyond the fields we know, somewhere that is beautiful beyond telling.

Someday not only will we become beautiful, the whole creation will become beautiful (Romans 8:18-22). *Stunningly* beautiful. For eye has not seen, nor ear heard, nor mind imagined all that God has prepared for those who love Him (1 Corinthians 2:9). The beauty of the most breathtaking mountains here is but a shadow of what awaits us there.

John Muir believed that God did His best work in the mountains. He wrote that "the rocks where the exposure to storms is the greatest, and where only ruin seems to be the object, are all the more lavished upon with beauty."

I pray this happens to my friends who so tragically lost their son. I have seen wonderful changes take place in their lives over the course of our thirty-year friendship. Every year a little more of Jesus emerges from their lives.

THE CONTINUING LANDSCAPE OF FAITH

A little more of His devotion. A little more of His wisdom. A little more of His compassion.

I don't understand how beauty could come from such a devastating experience as the one they have endured. I believe, though, that one day it *will* come. I hope to be there when it does, that I may stand before them with the same awe that filled John Muir as he stood before a mountain rising from the Columbia River basin. Transfixed by what he saw, Muir wrote:

> The whole mountain appeared as one glorious manifestation of divine power, enthusiastic and benevolent, glowing like a countenance with ineffable repose and beauty before which we could only gaze in devout and lowly admiration.

My eyes already touch the sunny hill,
going far ahead of the road I have begun.
So we are grasped by what we cannot grasp;
it has its inner light, even from a distance—

and changes us, even if we do not reach it,
into something else, which, hardly sensing it, we
    already are;
a gesture waves us on, answering our own wave ...
but what we feel is the wind in our faces.

Rainer Maria Rilke
From his poem, "The Walk"
March 1924

EPILOGUE

On a day in the mid-October of my life, I hiked to the Palmer Lake Reservoir, whose trail starts at the foothills of the Front Range. The reservoir has been formed by a concave wall of reinforced concrete that joins one mountain to the next, holding back a lake of water that has melted from countless mountaintops before it has found its way here.

I first hiked the reservoir for curiosity. Then, for exercise. Now I go for solitude. For a place to rest. A place to think. A place to pray.

Getting to that place, though, isn't easy. I trudge up a dirt road that is flung like a slender brown shawl around the mountain's pink, granite shoulders. The runoff from the reservoir, which was a torrent in spring, is down to a trickle. As it flows down the ravine, it babbles beautifully over the rocks, the way French is beautiful, full of soft,

THE WEATHERING GRACE OF GOD

gliding syllables cascading into mysterious words.

A touch of sun turns the landscape into a Maxfield Parrish painting. But this vibrant spill of eternity does not last. The light climbs the peaks, leaving shadows in its tracks, and reaching the peaks, disappears.

The sun sets on the town of Palmer Lake, which rises 7,200 feet above sea level. The reservoir is several hundred feet higher. As I make my way there, I grow tired. Certainly more tired than I was thirtysomething years ago when I was a teenager in good shape with good knees. I could have run the reservoir back then. Now I walk. Every so often I stop to catch my breath, to wipe the perspiration from my face, to ease the burn in my legs.

Each step, however tiring, takes me a little closer to the reservoir. I find strength in that. I also find a memory. The memory is an illustration in a sermon I once read by Vincent van Gogh. In that illustration is a prayer that has become *my* prayer for this stretch of my spiritual journey.

EPILOGUE

Especially at those times when life seems so endlessly uphill.

Van Gogh is known for his paintings, not his sermons, yet one led to the other as naturally as spring leads to summer. His first pastorate was in a tumbledown town of coal miners, where he lived among them, sharing their poverty, going with them into the mines and into their homes, tending the sick and conducting Sunday services. The sermon I'm thinking about is one he preached in 1877. As the text for his message, he used a biblical passage that compared life to a pilgrimage. He told the weary miners that they were strangers on this earth, that all of us were strangers on this earth, fellow travelers on our way home.

Van Gogh talked about the joys and sorrows of that journey, then used a painting of an autumn landscape to illustrate his point. In the distance a row of mountains stood hazed in dusk. The peaks splayed the setting sun, whose rays touched the underbellies of clouds, turning

common silver to gold and gold to royal purple. The leaves of the landscape were yellow, like the late-September leaves of Colorado aspen. A road, much like the one I'm traveling, cut through the landscape to a distant mountain. Crowning the mountain was a city, glowing in the sunset.

On the road was a weary traveler, van Gogh told them, staff in hand, who encountered an angel that had been placed there to encourage those on their way to the eternal city. Then van Gogh gave the words that he imagined might have passed between them.

The traveler asked: "Does the road go uphill all the way?"

The angel answered: "Yes, to the very end."

And he asked again: "And will the journey take all day long?"

The angel said: "From morn till night, my friend."

The traveler journeyed on, sorrowful yet rejoicing. Sorrowful because the road was so steep and long.

EPILOGUE

Rejoicing because he was closer to the destination that was home to his deepest longings. As he continued the climb, a quiet prayer rose from his lips:

"Then I shall be more and more tired ... but also nearer and nearer to Thee."

THE WEATHERING GRACE OF GOD

Dear Lord,

Help me in suffering my cross
to look to you and gain strength from how you
suffered yours,
to bear the pain of my unanswered
questions the way you bore yours.
Help me to see that even in the darkness and the
aloneness of your forsakenness,
still you loved,
still you forgave,
still you trusted yourself to the care of
your Father's hands.
Sometimes, Jesus, the road to the Father's house
seems so long and so steep
and sometimes I get so tired.

EPILOGUE

Here and there I need an angel, Lord,
*   someone along the way to lift my head,*
*   to point the way,*
*   and to tell me the truth about the road ahead.*

Grant me traveling mercies for the journey, Lord.
Help me to be as hopeful in my joy
*   as I am honest in my sorrow.*

Sorrowful but always rejoicing,
*   knowing that though I shall be more and more tired,*
*   I shall also be nearer and nearer to Thee.*

CREDITS